A D V E N T

GOSPEL

R E F L E C T I O N S

BISHOP ROBERT BARRON

WITH REFLECTION QUESTIONS BY
PEGGY PANDALEON

Published by Word on Fire, Elk Grove Village, IL 60007
© 2024 by Word on Fire Catholic Ministries
Printed in the United States of America
All rights reserved

Cover design by Cassie Bielak, typesetting by Marlene Burrell,
and interior art direction by Cassie Bielak and Katherine Spitler

ISBN: 978-1-68578-109-5

Library of Congress Control Number: 2023946611

INTRODUCTION

Friends,

Welcome to this great Advent journey! I'm so glad you're joining me and hundreds of thousands of others in prayer and reflection during this holy season.

Every Advent, Christians sing a haunting song whose words go back to the ninth century. But I wonder how carefully we listen to the lyrics:

> O come, O come, Emmanuel,
> and ransom captive Israel
> that mourns in lonely exile here
> until the Son of God appears.

In the ancient world, people were tremendously afraid of being kidnapped and held for ransom. Alone, far from home, malnourished, often tortured, hostages could only hope against hope that their deliverance might come. This is the situation evoked by that well-known song: Israel, the people of God, are held for ransom in their lonely exile, and they cry out for their Savior, the Son of God.

To be caught in the nexus of sin is to know the truth and to feel the texture of this imprisonment. We mourn over the sins and moral failures of our leaders; we feel trapped by our own falls into dysfunction and addiction; we feel overwhelmed by the dark powers of the world.

But the good news of Christianity is that *Emmanuel* (God with us) has indeed appeared, and he has gone right to the bottom of sin in order to defeat it. In his full humanity, Jesus entered into that complex web of sin, and in his full divinity, he did something about it.

May we spend these holy days together in prayer, penance, and hope, fixing our eyes on the appearance of Christ our Savior and longing for his deliverance.

God bless you,

+ Robert Barron

Bishop Robert Barron

ADVENT

GOSPEL

REFLECTIONS

DECEMBER 1, 2024

First Sunday of Advent

Luke 21:25–28, 34–36

Jesus said to his disciples: "There will be signs in the sun, the moon, and the stars, and on earth nations will be in dismay, perplexed by the roaring of the sea and the waves. People will die of fright in anticipation of what is coming upon the world, for the powers of the heavens will be shaken. And then they will see the Son of Man coming in a cloud with power and great glory. But when these signs begin to happen, stand erect and raise your heads because your redemption is at hand.

"Beware that your hearts do not become drowsy from carousing and drunkenness and the anxieties of daily life, and that day catch you by surprise like a trap. For that day will assault everyone who lives on the face of the earth. Be vigilant at all times and pray that you have the strength to escape the tribulations that are imminent and to stand before the Son of Man."

Friends, in today's Gospel, Jesus tells his disciples to be vigilant. Today marks the beginning of Advent, the great liturgical season of vigilance, of waiting and watching.

What practically can we do during this season of vigil keeping? What are some practices that might incarnate for us the Advent spirituality?

I strongly recommend the classically Catholic discipline of Eucharistic Adoration. To spend a half hour or an hour in the presence of the Lord is not to accomplish or achieve very much—it is not really "getting" anywhere—but it is a particularly rich form of spiritual waiting.

As you keep vigil before the Blessed Sacrament, bring to Christ some problem or dilemma that you have been fretting over, and then say, "Lord, I'm waiting for you to solve this, to show me the way out, the way forward. I've been running, planning, worrying, but now I'm going to let you work." Then, throughout Advent, watch attentively for signs.

Also, when you pray before the Eucharist, allow your desire for the things of God to intensify; allow your heart and soul to expand. Pray, "Lord, make me ready to receive the gifts you want to give," or even, "Lord Jesus, surprise me."

Reflect: In what ways do you plan to be vigilant this Advent season?

_____

_____

DECEMBER 2, 2024

Monday of the First Week of Advent

Matthew 8:5–11

When Jesus entered Capernaum, a centurion approached him and appealed to him, saying, "Lord, my servant is lying at home paralyzed, suffering dreadfully." He said to him, "I will come and cure him." The centurion said in reply, "Lord, I am not worthy to have you enter under my roof; only say the word and my servant will be healed. For I too am a man subject to authority, with soldiers subject to me. And I say to one, 'Go,' and he goes; and to another, 'Come here,' and he comes; and to my slave, 'Do this,' and he does it." When Jesus heard this, he was amazed and said to those following him, "Amen, I say to you, in no one in Israel have I found such faith. I say to you, many will come from the east and the west, and will recline with Abraham, Isaac, and Jacob at the banquet in the Kingdom of heaven."

Friends, in today's Gospel, Jesus celebrates the trust of the centurion who asked him to heal his servant: "Amen, I say to you, in no one in Israel have I found such faith."

We can say with the centurion that the Lord is a rock, a stronghold, a firm place to stand. The God who is not one more shifting and indefinite creature but rather the ground of being itself is a power upon whom we can rely, a covenant-maker whose word we can trust.

In his very freedom and sovereignty as our Creator, God is a parent in whose lap we can serenely find our rest. Undoubtedly, what has made religious belief such an indispensable part of human consciousness and behavior is just this assurance of safety that it brings.

There is nothing in the cosmos that will not, finally, disappoint us. There is no place in the universe that will not, finally, be shaken. But God, the self-sufficient ground of existence itself, can be trusted not to disappoint and not to betray. "No storm can shake my inmost calm, while to that rock I'm clinging," says the author of the Shaker hymn, witnessing ecstatically to this divine faithfulness.

Reflect: Have you ever, as the centurion, gone beyond reason and relied on faith?

DECEMBER 3, 2024

Luke 10:21–24

Jesus rejoiced in the Holy Spirit and said, "I give you praise, Father, Lord of heaven and earth, for although you have hidden these things from the wise and the learned you have revealed them to the childlike. Yes, Father, such has been your gracious will. All things have been handed over to me by my Father. No one knows who the Son is except the Father, and who the Father is except the Son and anyone to whom the Son wishes to reveal him."

Turning to the disciples in private he said, "Blessed are the eyes that see what you see. For I say to you, many prophets and kings desired to see what you see, but did not see it, and to hear what you hear, but did not hear it."

Friends, in today's Gospel, Jesus places a high value on child-likeness. What is it about "the childlike" that Jesus prizes? Jesus himself *is* the child, the Son who has received everything from his Father. He lives in an attitude of receptivity, taking in all that the Father has given him. His is a life of obedience. He is not in command of his life, but he receives it as a gift.

This is what it means to be a little child: to have an attitude of receptivity that allows you to be moved by God and by God's ways. The problem with "the wise and the learned" is not that they're educated, but that they are trying to govern and run their own lives on their own terms rather than living in obedience to God. The truly wise are those who are like Christ: little children in relation to God.

Reflect: How do you need to be more like a child and look to God to receive all that he wants to give you?

_____

_____

_____

_____

_____

_____

_____

_____

_____

_____

_____

_____

DECEMBER 4, 2024

Wednesday of the First Week of Advent

Matthew 15:29–37

At that time, Jesus walked by the Sea of Galilee, went up on the mountain, and sat down there. Great crowds came to him, having with them the lame, the blind, the deformed, the mute, and many others. They placed them at his feet, and he cured them. The crowds were amazed when they saw the mute speaking, the deformed made whole, the lame walking, and the blind able to see, and they glorified the God of Israel.

Jesus summoned his disciples and said, "My heart is moved with pity for the crowd, for they have been with me now for three days and have nothing to eat. I do not want to send them away hungry, for fear they may collapse on the way." The disciples said to him, "Where could we ever get enough bread in this deserted place to satisfy such a crowd?" Jesus said to them, "How many loaves do you have?" "Seven," they replied, "and a few fish." He ordered the crowd to sit down on the ground. Then he took the seven loaves and the fish, gave thanks, broke the loaves, and gave them to the disciples, who in turn gave them to the crowds. They all ate and were satisfied. They picked up the fragments left over—seven baskets full.

Friends, in today's Gospel, Jesus instructs the crowd to sit on the ground. Taking the seven loaves and a few fish, he makes a meal that satisfies the enormous crowd. They are hungry, tired, and worn out from their exertions, and Jesus gives them sustenance for the day.

For Thomas Aquinas, the great metaphor for the Eucharist is sustenance, food for the journey. The Eucharist is daily food, nourishment to get us through the day-to-day. How effective would we be if we never ate, or ate only on special occasions and in a festive environment? Not very. So, in the spiritual life, we must eat and drink or we will not have strength.

Is this just meant in some vague symbolic way? No, rather in a vividly analogical way. For just as the body needs physical nourishment, the spirit needs spiritual nourishment, and there is no getting around this law.

Sometimes we think it's no big deal if we stay away from Mass and refrain from receiving Communion. Not so, according to the spiritual physics laid out in this account.

Reflect: Is the Eucharist true *sustenance* or just a *symbol* for you? Do you notice any change in your life when you don't receive Communion for a while?

_____

_____

_____

_____

_____

_____

_____

_____

_____

_____

_____

_____

_____

_____

_____

_____

_____

DECEMBER 5, 2024

Thursday of the First Week of Advent

Matthew 7:21, 24–27

Jesus said to his disciples: "Not everyone who says to me, 'Lord, Lord,' will enter the Kingdom of heaven, but only the one who does the will of my Father in heaven.

"Everyone who listens to these words of mine and acts on them will be like a wise man who built his house on rock. The rain fell, the floods came, and the winds blew and buffeted the house. But it did not collapse; it had been set solidly on rock. And everyone who listens to these words of mine but does not act on them will be like a fool who built his house on sand. The rain fell, the floods came, and the winds blew and buffeted the house. And it collapsed and was completely ruined."

Friends, in today's Gospel, Jesus closes his Sermon on the Mount by showing us the importance of applying his teaching: "Everyone who listens to these words of mine and acts on them will be like a wise man who built his house on rock. The rain fell, the floods came, and the winds blew and buffeted the house. But it did not collapse."

This is the heart of it: if you are rooted in God, then you can withstand anything, precisely because you are linked to that power which is creating the cosmos. You will be blessed at the deepest place, and nothing can finally touch you.

But the one who does not take Jesus' words to heart "will be like the fool who built his house on sand. The rain fell, the floods came, and the winds buffeted the house. And it collapsed and was completely ruined." When the inevitable trials come, the life built on pleasure, money, power, or fame will give way.

So the question is a simple one: Where do you stand? How goes it with your heart? On what, precisely, is the whole of your life built?

Reflect: Which commands of Jesus have you listened to and acted upon? Which have you listened to but not acted upon, thereby weakening your "foundation"?

DECEMBER 6, 2024

Friday of the First Week of Advent

Matthew 9:27–31

As Jesus passed by, two blind men followed him, crying out, "Son of David, have pity on us!" When he entered the house, the blind men approached him and Jesus said to them, "Do you believe that I can do this?" "Yes, Lord," they said to him. Then he touched their eyes and said, "Let it be done for you according to your faith." And their eyes were opened. Jesus warned them sternly, "See that no one knows about this." But they went out and spread word of him through all that land.

Friends, today in our Gospel, two blind men beg Jesus to heal them.

Blindness in the Bible is very often a symbol of spiritual blindness: the incapacity to see what truly matters. Focused on the worldly goods of wealth, pleasure, power, and honor, most people don't see how blind they are to the truly important things: giving oneself to the grace of God and living a life of love. If you have not surrendered to the grace of God, you are blind. How wonderful it is, then, that these men in the Gospel can cry out to Jesus in their need.

They are, of course, making a petition for physical healing, but it's much more than that for us. It's asking for that one thing that finally matters: spiritual vision—to know what my life is about, to know the big picture, to know where I'm going. You can have all the wealth, pleasure, honor, and power you want. You can have all the worldly goods you could desire. But if you don't see spiritually, it will do you no good; it will probably destroy you.

Reflect: What worldly attachments are most often blocking your spiritual vision and your willingness to surrender to God's grace?

_____

_____

_____

_____

_____

_____

_____

_____

_____

_____

_____

DECEMBER 7, 2024

Matthew 9:35–10:1, 5a, 6–8

Jesus went around to all the towns and villages, teaching in their synagogues, proclaiming the Gospel of the Kingdom, and curing every disease and illness. At the sight of the crowds, his heart was moved with pity for them because they were troubled and abandoned, like sheep without a shepherd. Then he said to his disciples, "The harvest is abundant but the laborers are few; so ask the master of the harvest to send out laborers for his harvest."

Then he summoned his Twelve disciples and gave them authority over unclean spirits to drive them out and to cure every disease and every illness.

Jesus sent out these Twelve after instructing them thus, "Go to the lost sheep of the house of Israel. As you go, make this proclamation: 'The Kingdom of heaven is at hand.' Cure the sick, raise the dead, cleanse lepers, drive out demons. Without cost you have received; without cost you are to give."

Friends, today Jesus instructs us to pray for laborers for the harvest, for disciples to do the work of evangelization. We need to organize our lives around evangelization. Everything we do ought to be related somehow to it. This doesn't mean that we all have to become professional evangelizers. Remember, you can evangelize by the moral quality of your life. But it does mean that nothing in our lives ought to be more important than announcing the victory of Jesus.

We should think of others not as objects to be used, or annoying people in the way of realizing our projects, but rather as those whom we are called to serve. Instead of saying, "Why is this annoying person in my way?" we should ask, "What opportunity for evangelization has presented itself?" Has God put this person in your life precisely for this purpose?

Reflect: In what ways do you "announce the victory of Jesus" in your life?

DECEMBER 8, 2024

Luke 3:1–6

In the fifteenth year of the reign of Tiberius Caesar, when Pontius Pilate was governor of Judea, and Herod was tetrarch of Galilee, and his brother Philip tetrarch of the region of Ituraea and Trachonitis, and Lysanias was tetrarch of Abilene, during the high priesthood of Annas and Caiaphas, the word of God came to John the son of Zechariah in the desert. John went throughout the whole region of the Jordan, proclaiming a baptism of repentance for the forgiveness of sins, as it is written in the book of the words of the prophet Isaiah:

A voice of one crying out in the desert:
"Prepare the way of the Lord,
make straight his paths.
Every valley shall be filled
and every mountain and hill shall be made low.
The winding roads shall be made straight,
and the rough ways made smooth,
and all flesh shall see the salvation of God."

Friends, in today's Gospel, Luke quotes from the prophet Isaiah:

> "Prepare the way of the Lord,
>   make straight his paths." (Isa. 40:3)

Advent is a great liturgical season of waiting—but not a passive waiting. We yearn, we search, and we reach out for the God who will come to us in human flesh. In short, we prepare the way of the Lord Jesus Christ.

This preparation has a penitential dimension, because it is the season in which we prepare for the coming of a Savior, and we don't need a Savior unless we're deeply convinced there is something to be saved from. When we have become deeply aware of our sin, we know that we can cling to nothing in ourselves, that everything we offer is, to some degree, tainted and impure. We can't show our cultural, professional, and personal accomplishments to God as though they are enough to save us. But the moment we realize that fact, we move into the Advent spirit, desperately craving a Savior.

In the book of Isaiah (Isa. 64:8), we read:

> "Yet, O LORD, you are our father;
>   we are the clay and you the potter:
>   we are all the work of your hands."

Today, let us prepare ourselves for the potter to come.

Reflect: Are you spiritually passive or active this Advent as you wait for the coming of Jesus? How can you become more spiritually active amid the busyness of the season?

DECEMBER 9, 2024

Solemnity of the Immaculate Conception of the Blessed Virgin Mary

Luke 1:26–38

The angel Gabriel was sent from God to a town of Galilee called Nazareth, to a virgin betrothed to a man named Joseph, of the house of David, and the virgin's name was Mary. And coming to her, he said, "Hail, full of grace! The Lord is with you." But she was greatly troubled at what was said and pondered what sort of greeting this might be. Then the angel said to her, "Do not be afraid, Mary, for you have found favor with God. Behold, you will conceive in your womb and bear a son, and you shall name him Jesus. He will be great and will be called Son of the Most High, and the Lord God will give him the throne of David his father, and he will rule over the house of Jacob forever, and of his Kingdom there will be no end." But Mary said to the angel, "How can this be, since I have no relations with a man?" And the angel said to her in reply, "The Holy Spirit will come upon you, and the power of the Most High will overshadow you. Therefore the child to be born will be called holy, the Son of God. And behold, Elizabeth, your relative, has also

conceived a son in her old age, and this is the sixth
month for her who was called barren; for nothing
will be impossible for God." Mary said, "Behold, I
am the handmaid of the Lord. May it be done to me
according to your word." Then the angel departed
from her.

Friends, today we celebrate the Solemnity of the Immaculate
Conception of the Blessed Virgin Mary.

In 1854, Pope Pius IX declared the dogma of the Immaculate
Conception—the truth that Mary, through a special grace, was
preserved free from original sin from the first moment of her
conception.

Were this not the case, the angel would not have referred to her
at the Annunciation as *Kecharitomene* (full of grace). Why would
God do such a thing? And wouldn't this imply that Mary does
not need to be redeemed?

The traditional answer is that God wanted to prepare a worthy
vessel for the reception of his Word. Just as the Holy of Holies in
the temple was kept pure and inviolate, so the definitive Temple,
the true Ark of the Covenant, which is Mary herself, should all
the more be untrammeled.

Bl. John Duns Scotus explained that Mary is indeed redeemed
by the grace of her Son, but since that grace exists outside of

time, it can be applied in a way that transcends the ordinary rhythms of time. Therefore, Mary, by a kind of preemptive strike, was delivered by Christ's grace from original sin.

Reflect: What role does the Blessed Virgin Mary play in your life?

_____

_____

_____

_____

_____

_____

_____

_____

_____

_____

_____

_____

_____

_____

_____

DECEMBER 10, 2024

Matthew 18:12–14

Jesus said to his disciples: "What is your opinion? If a man has a hundred sheep and one of them goes astray, will he not leave the ninety-nine in the hills and go in search of the stray? And if he finds it, amen, I say to you, he rejoices more over it than over the ninety-nine that did not stray. In just the same way, it is not the will of your heavenly Father that one of these little ones be lost."

Friends, in today's Gospel, Jesus asks: "If a man has a hundred sheep and one of them goes astray, will he not leave the ninety-nine in the hills and go in search of the stray?" Well, of course not! No self-respecting shepherd would ever think of doing that. If you were a shepherd, you'd cut your losses. That sheep is probably dead anyway if it wandered far enough away.

But we are to understand that God is like that foolish shepherd. God's love throws caution to the wind to seek out the lost sheep. We might expect God to be good to those who are good, and kind to those who follow his commandments. Those who don't, who wander away, are simply lost. God might give them a few minutes, but then they're on their own.

No, God is like this kooky shepherd. God loves irrationally, exuberantly risking it all in order to find the one who wandered away. What good news: God does not love according to a strict justice on our terms but loves in his own extravagant way.

Reflect: Meditate on a time when you were the one lost sheep and received the extravagant, irrational love of God.

DECEMBER 11, 2024

Wednesday of the Second Week of Advent

Matthew 11:28–30

Jesus said to the crowds: "Come to me, all you who labor and are burdened, and I will give you rest. Take my yoke upon you and learn from me, for I am meek and humble of heart; and you will find rest for yourselves. For my yoke is easy, and my burden light."

Friends, in today's Gospel, Jesus offers to free us from the burden of our pride.

What is it that makes our lives heavy and weighed down? Precisely the burden of our own egos, the weight of one's own self. When I am puffing myself up with my own self-importance, I'm laboring under all that weight. Jesus is saying, "Become a child. Take that weight off your shoulders and put on the weight of my yoke, the yoke of my obedience to the Father."

Anthony de Mello proposed the following parable to describe us prideful souls. A group of people sit on a bus that is passing through the most glorious countryside, but they have the shades pulled down on all the windows and are bickering about who gets front seat on the bus. This is the burden of pride: preferring the narrow and stuffy confines of the bus to the beauty that is effortlessly available all around. This, of course, is why Jesus can say, "My yoke is easy, and my burden is light." What the Lord proposes is not a freedom from suffering but, what is much more important, a freedom from the self.

Reflect: From your own experience, explain how true freedom is "easy" when yoked to Christ.

_____

_____

_____

_____

_____

_____

_____

_____

_____

_____

_____

_____

_____

_____

DECEMBER 12, 2024

Feast of Our Lady of Guadalupe

Luke 1:26–38 (or Luke 1:39–47)

The angel Gabriel was sent from God to a town of Galilee called Nazareth, to a virgin betrothed to a man named Joseph, of the house of David, and the virgin's name was Mary. And coming to her, he said, "Hail, full of grace! The Lord is with you." But she was greatly troubled at what was said and pondered what sort of greeting this might be. Then the angel said to her, "Do not be afraid, Mary, for you have found favor with God. Behold, you will conceive in your womb and bear a son, and you shall name him Jesus. He will be great and will be called Son of the Most High, and the Lord God will give him the throne of David his father, and he will rule over the house of Jacob forever, and of his Kingdom there will be no end." But Mary said to the angel, "How can this be, since I have no relations with a man?" And the angel said to her in reply, "The Holy Spirit will come upon you, and the power of the Most High will overshadow you. Therefore the child to be born will be called holy, the Son of God. And behold, Elizabeth, your relative, has also conceived a son in her old age, and this is the sixth month for her who was called barren; for nothing will be impossible for God." Mary said, "Behold, I am the handmaid of the Lord. May it be done to me according to your word." Then the angel departed from her.

Friends, today we celebrate the great feast of Our Lady of Guadalupe. What followed the apparition of Mary at Tepeyac is one of the most astounding chapters in the history of Christian evangelization.

Though Franciscan missionaries had been laboring in Mexico for twenty years, they had made little progress. But within ten years of the appearance of Our Lady of Guadalupe practically the entire Mexican people, nine million strong, had converted to Christianity. Our Lady of Guadalupe had proved a more effective evangelist than Peter, Paul, St. Patrick, and St. Francis Xavier combined! And with that great national conversion, the Aztec practice of human sacrifice came to an end. She had done battle with fallen spirits and had won a culture-changing victory for the God of love.

The challenge for us who honor her today is to join the same fight. We must announce to our culture today the truth of the God of Israel, the God of Jesus Christ, the God of nonviolence and forgiving love. And we ought, like Our Lady of Guadalupe, to be bearers of Jesus to a world that needs him more than ever.

Reflect: In what ways does our culture "sacrifice humans," either literally or figuratively? What is your responsibility as a disciple of Christ to work to put an end to these affronts to human dignity?

DECEMBER 13, 2024

Memorial of Saint Lucy, Virgin and Martyr

Matthew 11:16–19

Jesus said to the crowds: "To what shall I compare this generation? It is like children who sit in marketplaces and call to one another, 'We played the flute for you, but you did not dance, we sang a dirge but you did not mourn.' For John came neither eating nor drinking, and they said, 'He is possessed by a demon.' The Son of Man came eating and drinking and they said, 'Look, he is a glutton and a drunkard, a friend of tax collectors and sinners.' But wisdom is vindicated by her works."

Friends, in today's Gospel, Jesus says, "The Son of Man came eating and drinking and they said, 'Look, he is a glutton and a drunkard, a friend of tax collectors and sinners.'"

The Passover meal was decisively important in salvation history. God commands that his people share a meal to remember their liberation from slavery. This supper provides the context for the deepest theologizing of the Israelite community. Both the bitterness of their slavery and the sweetness of their liberation are acted out in this sacred meal.

Jesus' life and ministry can be interpreted in light of this symbol. From the very beginning, Jesus was laid in a manger, for he would be food for a hungry world. Much of Jesus' public outreach centered on sacred meals, where everyone was invited: rich and poor, saints and sinners, the sick and the outcast. They thought John the Baptist was a weird ascetic, but they called Jesus a glutton and a winebibber. He embodies Yahweh's desire to eat a convivial meal with his people.

And of course, the life and teaching of Jesus comes to a sort of climax at the meal that we call the Last Supper. The Eucharist is what we do in the in-between times, between the Ascension of the Lord and his coming in glory. It is the meal that even now anticipates the perfect meal of fellowship with God.

Reflect: How does Jesus' statement that "wisdom is vindicated by her works" take the sting out of the crowd's accusations?

_____

_____

_____

_____

_____

_____

_____

_____

_____

DECEMBER 14, 2024

Memorial of Saint John of the Cross, Priest and Doctor of the Church

Matthew 17:9a, 10–13

As they were coming down from the mountain, the disciples asked Jesus, "Why do the scribes say that Elijah must come first?" He said in reply, "Elijah will indeed come and restore all things; but I tell you that Elijah has already come, and they did not recognize him but did to him whatever they pleased. So also will the Son of Man suffer at their hands." Then the disciples understood that he was speaking to them of John the Baptist.

Friends, today we celebrate the memorial of the great Spanish mystic St. John of the Cross.

We find ourselves, St. John of the Cross taught, in the midst of a good and beautiful world, but we are meant finally for union with God. Therefore, the soul has to become free from its attachments to finite things so as to be free for communion with God.

This purification first involves what John called "the night of the senses" (the letting go of physical and sensual pleasures), and it continues with "the night of the soul" (a detachment from the mental images that one can use as a substitute for God).

Like all purifications, this one is painful, especially if one's attachment to these finite things is intense. It will often manifest itself, John of the Cross said, as dryness in prayer and a keen sense of the absence and even abandonment of God.

In this process, God is not toying with the soul; rather, he is performing a kind of surgery upon it, cutting certain things away so that its life might intensify.

Reflect: Have you ever experienced dryness in prayer or the sense of being abandoned by God? How does your faith carry you through these times?

DECEMBER 15, 2024

Third Sunday of Advent

Luke 3:10–18

The crowds asked John the Baptist, "What should we do?" He said to them in reply, "Whoever has two cloaks should share with the person who has none. And whoever has food should do likewise." Even tax collectors came to be baptized and they said to him, "Teacher, what should we do?" He answered them, "Stop collecting more than what is prescribed." Soldiers also asked him, "And what is it that we should do?" He told them, "Do not practice extortion, do not falsely accuse anyone, and be satisfied with your wages."

Now the people were filled with expectation, and all were asking in their hearts whether John might be the Christ. John answered them all, saying, "I am baptizing you with water, but one mightier than I is coming. I am not worthy to loosen the thongs of his sandals. He will baptize you with the Holy Spirit and fire. His winnowing fan is in his hand to clear

> his threshing floor and to gather the wheat into his barn, but the chaff he will burn with unquenchable fire." Exhorting them in many other ways, he preached good news to the people.

Friends, like those in the time of John the Baptist, we ask: "What should we do?" How should we live our lives?

This question, of course, tells us something else about repentance: that it has to do with action more than simply changing our minds. The spiritual life is, finally, a set of behaviors.

So what does John the Baptist tell us to do? His first recommendation is this: "Whoever has two cloaks should share with the person who has none." This is so basic, so elemental—yet so almost thoroughly ignored! In the Church's social teaching, we find a constant reminder that although private property is a social good, the use of our private property must always have a social orientation.

An early Church Father, St. Basil the Great, expressed the idea in tones that echo John the Baptist: "The bread in your cupboard belongs to the hungry. The cloak in your wardrobe belongs to the naked. The shoes you allow to rot belong to the barefoot. The money in your vaults belongs to the destitute. You do injustice to every man whom you could help but do not."

So what should we do this Advent, we who seek repentance, we who await the coming of the Messiah? Serve justice, render to each his due, and give to those who are in need.

Reflect: How do you use your private property for the common good?

_____

_____

_____

_____

_____

_____

_____

_____

_____

_____

_____

_____

_____

_____

DECEMBER 16, 2024

Monday of the Third Week of Advent

Matthew 21:23–27

When Jesus had come into the temple area, the chief priests and the elders of the people approached him as he was teaching and said, "By what authority are you doing these things? And who gave you this authority?" Jesus said to them in reply, "I shall ask you one question, and if you answer it for me, then I shall tell you by what authority I do these things. Where was John's baptism from? Was it of heavenly or of human origin?" They discussed this among themselves and said, "If we say 'Of heavenly origin,' he will say to us, 'Then why did you not believe him?' But if we say, 'Of human origin,' we fear the crowd, for they all regard John as a prophet." So they said to Jesus in reply, "We do not know." He himself said to them, "Neither shall I tell you by what authority I do these things."

Friends, in today's Gospel, the chief priests and elders question Jesus: "By what authority are you doing these things? And who gave you this authority?"

The Greek word used for "authority" is most enlightening: *exousia*. It means, literally, "from the being of." Jesus speaks with the very *exousia* of God, and therefore, his words effect what they say. He says, "Lazarus, come out!" (John 11:43), and the dead man comes out of the tomb. He rebukes the wind and says to the sea, "Be still!" (Mark 4:39), and there is calm. And the night before he dies, he takes bread and says, "This is my body" (Matt. 26:26; Mark 14:22; Luke 22:19). And what he says is.

Friends, this is the authority of the Church. If we are simply the guardians of one interesting philosophical perspective among many, then we are powerless. If we rely on our own cleverness in argumentation, then we will fail. Our power comes—and this remains a great mystery—only when we speak with the authority of Jesus Christ.

Reflect: How can the Church, or any of its members, "speak with the authority of Jesus Christ"?

_____

_____

_____

_____

_____

_____

_____

_____

DECEMBER 17, 2024

Tuesday of the Third Week of Advent

Matthew 1:1–17

The book of the genealogy of Jesus Christ, the son of David, the son of Abraham.

Abraham became the father of Isaac, Isaac the father of Jacob, Jacob the father of Judah and his brothers. Judah became the father of Perez and Zerah, whose mother was Tamar. Perez became the father of Hezron, Hezron the father of Ram, Ram the father of Amminadab. Amminadab became the father of Nahshon, Nahshon the father of Salmon, Salmon the father of Boaz, whose mother was Rahab. Boaz became the father of Obed, whose mother was Ruth. Obed became the father of Jesse, Jesse the father of David the king.

David became the father of Solomon, whose mother had been the wife of Uriah. Solomon became the father of Rehoboam, Rehoboam the father of Abijah, Abijah the father of Asaph. Asaph became the father of Jehoshaphat, Jehoshaphat the father of Joram, Joram the father of Uzziah. Uzziah became the father of Jotham, Jotham the father of Ahaz,

Ahaz the father of Hezekiah. Hezekiah became the father of Manasseh, Manasseh the father of Amos, Amos the father of Josiah. Josiah became the father of Jechoniah and his brothers at the time of the Babylonian exile.

After the Babylonian exile, Jechoniah became the father of Shealtiel, Shealtiel the father of Zerubbabel, Zerubbabel the father of Abiud. Abiud became the father of Eliakim, Eliakim the father of Azor, Azor the father of Zadok. Zadok became the father of Achim, Achim the father of Eliud, Eliud the father of Eleazar. Eleazar became the father of Matthan, Matthan the father of Jacob, Jacob the father of Joseph, the husband of Mary. Of her was born Jesus who is called the Christ.

Thus the total number of generations from Abraham to David is fourteen generations; from David to the Babylonian exile, fourteen generations; from the Babylonian exile to the Christ, fourteen generations.

Friends, today's Gospel records the genealogy of Jesus. It was desperately important for Matthew to show that Jesus didn't just appear out of the blue. Rather, he came out of a rich, densely textured history. St. Irenaeus tells us that the Incarnation had been taking place over a long period of time, with God gradually accustoming himself to the human race.

Look at this long line of characters: saints, sinners, cheats, prostitutes, murderers, poets, kings, insiders, and outsiders—all leading to the Christ. Of course, King David is mentioned. He was, without doubt, a great figure, the king who united the nation. But he was also an adulterer and a murderer.

From this long line of the great and not-so-great, the prominent and obscure, saints and sinners, and kings and paupers came "Jesus who is called the Christ." God became one of us, in all of our grace and embarrassment, in all of our beauty and ordinariness. God had a series of human ancestors, and, like most families, they were kind of a mixed bag. And what good news this is for us! It means that God can bring the Christ to birth even in people like us.

Reflect: Think about your own family. Where have you seen God work in "the great and not-so-great"?

_____

_____

_____

_____

_____

_____

_____

_____

_____

DECEMBER 18, 2024

Wednesday of the Third Week of Advent

Matthew 1:18–25

This is how the birth of Jesus Christ came about. When his mother Mary was betrothed to Joseph, but before they lived together, she was found with child through the Holy Spirit. Joseph her husband, since he was a righteous man, yet unwilling to expose her to shame, decided to divorce her quietly. Such was his intention when, behold, the angel of the Lord appeared to him in a dream and said, "Joseph, son of David, do not be afraid to take Mary your wife into your home. For it is through the Holy Spirit that this child has been conceived in her. She will bear a son and you are to name him Jesus, because he will save his people from their sins." All this took place to fulfill what the Lord had said through the prophet:

> Behold, the virgin shall be with child and bear
> a son,
> and they shall name him Emmanuel,

which means "God is with us." When Joseph awoke, he did as the angel of the Lord had commanded

> him and took his wife into his home. He had no
> relations with her until she bore a son, and he
> named him Jesus.

Friends, in today's Gospel, an angel tells Joseph in a dream to name his son Jesus "because he will save his people from their sins."

Well, that's the Good News of Christmas. The rightful King has returned to reclaim what is his and to let the prisoners go free. The God announced by all the prophets and patriarchs—by Abraham, Jeremiah, Ezekiel, Amos, and Isaiah—is a God of justice, and this means that he burns to set things right. God hates the sin and violence and injustice that have rendered gloomy his beautiful world, and therefore he comes into that world as a warrior, ready to fight. But he arrives (and here is the delicious irony of Christmas) stealthily, clandestinely—sneaking, as it were, unnoticed behind enemy lines.

The King comes as a helpless infant, born of insignificant parents in a small town of a distant outpost of the Roman Empire. He will conquer through the finally irresistible power of love, the same power with which he made the universe.

Reflect: In what ways can you "conquer through the irresistible power of love" in the battles of your life?

DECEMBER 19, 2024

Thursday of the Third Week of Advent

Luke 1:5–25

In the days of Herod, King of Judea, there was a priest named Zechariah of the priestly division of Abijah; his wife was from the daughters of Aaron, and her name was Elizabeth. Both were righteous in the eyes of God, observing all the commandments and ordinances of the Lord blamelessly. But they had no child, because Elizabeth was barren and both were advanced in years.

Once when he was serving as priest in his division's turn before God, according to the practice of the priestly service, he was chosen by lot to enter the sanctuary of the Lord to burn incense. Then, when the whole assembly of the people was praying outside at the hour of the incense offering, the angel of the Lord appeared to him, standing at the right of the altar of incense. Zechariah was troubled by what he saw, and fear came upon him.

But the angel said to him, "Do not be afraid, Zechariah, because your prayer has been heard. Your wife Elizabeth will bear you a son, and you shall name him John. And you will have joy and gladness, and many will rejoice at his birth, for he will be great in the sight of the Lord. He will drink neither wine nor strong drink. He will be filled with the Holy Spirit even from his mother's womb, and he will turn many of the children of Israel to the Lord their God. He will go before him in the spirit and power of Elijah to turn the hearts of fathers toward children and the disobedient to the understanding of the righteous, to prepare a people fit for the Lord."

Then Zechariah said to the angel, "How shall I know this? For I am an old man, and my wife is advanced in years." And the angel said to him in reply, "I am Gabriel, who stand before God. I was sent to speak to you and to announce to you this good news. But now you will be speechless and unable to talk until the day these things take place, because you did not believe my words, which will be fulfilled at their proper time." Meanwhile the people were waiting for Zechariah and were amazed that he stayed so long in the sanctuary. But when he came out, he was unable to speak to them, and they realized that he had seen a vision in the sanctuary. He was gesturing to them but remained mute.

> Then, when his days of ministry were completed, he went home.
>
> After this time his wife Elizabeth conceived, and she went into seclusion for five months, saying, "So has the Lord done for me at a time when he has seen fit to take away my disgrace before others."

Friends, in today's Gospel, Luke tells us about John the Baptist's parents. We see with utter clarity that John is a priestly figure. Zechariah, his father, is a temple priest, and Elizabeth, his mother, is a descendant of Aaron, the very first priest.

Now flash forward thirty years and see John emerging in the desert. The first question is, "Why is this son of a priest not working in the temple?" And the second is, "Why are the people going out from Jerusalem to commune with him?" The answer to the first is that he is engaging in a prophetic critique of a temple that has gone bad. And the answer to the second is that he is performing the acts of a purified temple priest out in the desert. His baptism was a ritual cleansing and a spur to repent, precisely what a pious Jew would have sought in the temple.

And the picture becomes complete when Jesus arrives to be baptized, and John says, "Behold, the Lamb of God." This is explicitly temple talk. He is saying that the one who is to be sacrificed has arrived. He is the fulfillment of priesthood, temple, and sacrifice. The priestly figure has done his work, and now he fades away.

Reflect: How can truly living the Gospel today be as counter-cultural as John the Baptist was in his time?

_____

_____

_____

_____

_____

_____

_____

_____

_____

_____

_____

_____

_____

_____

_____

_____

DECEMBER 20, 2024

Friday of the Third Week of Advent

Luke 1:26–38

In the sixth month, the angel Gabriel was sent from God to a town of Galilee called Nazareth, to a virgin betrothed to a man named Joseph, of the house of David, and the virgin's name was Mary. And coming to her, he said, "Hail, full of grace! The Lord is with you." But she was greatly troubled at what was said and pondered what sort of greeting this might be. Then the angel said to her, "Do not be afraid, Mary, for you have found favor with God. Behold, you will conceive in your womb and bear a son, and you shall name him Jesus. He will be great and will be called Son of the Most High, and the Lord God will give him the throne of David his father, and he will rule over the house of Jacob forever, and of his Kingdom there will be no end."

But Mary said to the angel, "How can this be, since I have no relations with a man?" And the angel said to her in reply, "The Holy Spirit will come upon you, and the power of the Most High will overshadow you. Therefore the child to be born will be called holy, the Son of God. And behold, Elizabeth, your relative, has also conceived a son in her old age, and this is the sixth month for her who was called barren; for nothing will be impossible for God."

Mary said, "Behold, I am the handmaid of the Lord. May it be done to me according to your word." Then the angel departed from her.

Friends, today's Gospel declares the significance of Mary's *fiat*. When Mary says, "Behold, I am the handmaid of the Lord. May it be done to me according to your word," she exhibits such faith and thereby undoes the refusal of Eve. And this *fiat* to the impossible made possible the Incarnation of God. In accepting the seduction of the alluring Mystery, she allowed God's love to become enfleshed for the transformation of the world.

In the Catholic faith, Mary is praised as the Mother of the Church, the matrix of all discipleship. What this means is that her *fiat* is the ground and model of every disciple's response to God's desire for incarnation. Meister Eckhart said that all believers become "mothers of Christ," bearers of the incarnate Word, in the measure that they acquiesce to the divine passion to push concretely into creation.

Reflect: When have you said "yes" to God, not knowing the consequences or outcome of your obedience?

DECEMBER 21, 2024

Saturday of the Third Week of Advent

Luke 1:39–45

Mary set out in those days and traveled to the hill country in haste to a town of Judah, where she entered the house of Zechariah and greeted Elizabeth. When Elizabeth heard Mary's greeting, the infant leaped in her womb, and Elizabeth, filled with the Holy Spirit, cried out in a loud voice and said, "Most blessed are you among women, and blessed is the fruit of your womb. And how does this happen to me, that the mother of my Lord should come to me? For at the moment the sound of your greeting reached my ears, the infant in my womb leaped for joy. Blessed are you who believed that what was spoken to you by the Lord would be fulfilled."

Friends, today's Gospel tells the marvelous story of the Visitation. At the Annunciation, the angel had told Mary that the child to be conceived in her would be the new David.

With that magnificent prophecy still ringing in her ears, Mary set out to visit her cousin Elizabeth, who was married to Zechariah, a temple priest. No first-century Jew would have missed the significance of their residence being in "the hill country of Judah." That was precisely where David found the ark, the bearer of God's presence. To that same hill country now comes Mary, the definitive and final Ark of the Covenant.

Elizabeth is the first to proclaim the fullness of the Gospel: "How does this happen to me, that the mother of my Lord should come to me?"—the Lord, which is to say, the God of Israel. Mary brings God into the world, thus making it, at least in principle, a temple.

And then Elizabeth announces that at the sound of Mary's greeting, "the infant in my womb leaped for joy." This is the un- born John the Baptist doing his version of David's dance before the ark of the covenant, his great act of worship of the King.

Reflect: Can you feel the joy in this Gospel passage? When have you experienced such joy in your own faith life?

_____

_____

_____

_____

_____

_____

_____

_____

DECEMBER 22, 2024

Fourth Sunday of Advent

Luke 1:39–45

Mary set out in those days and traveled to the hill country in haste to a town of Judah, where she entered the house of Zechariah and greeted Elizabeth. When Elizabeth heard Mary's greeting, the infant leaped in her womb, and Elizabeth, filled with the Holy Spirit, cried out in a loud voice and said, "Most blessed are you among women, and blessed is the fruit of your womb. And how does this happen to me, that the mother of my Lord should come to me? For at the moment the sound of your greeting reached my ears, the infant in my womb leaped for joy. Blessed are you who believed that what was spoken to you by the Lord would be fulfilled."

Friends, today's Gospel again tells of Mary's visit to Elizabeth. I've always been fascinated by Mary's "haste" in this story of the Visitation. Upon hearing the message of Gabriel concerning her own pregnancy and that of her cousin, Mary proceeded "in haste" into the hill country of Judah to see Elizabeth.

Why did she go with such speed and purpose? Because she had found her mission, her role in the theo-drama. We are dominated today by the ego-drama in all of its ramifications and implications.

The ego-drama is the play that I'm writing, I'm producing, I'm directing, and I'm starring in. We see this absolutely everywhere in our culture. Freedom of choice reigns supreme; I become the person that I choose to be.

The theo-drama is the great story being told by God, the great play being directed by God. What makes life thrilling is to discover your role in it. This is precisely what has happened to Mary. She has found her role—indeed a climactic role—in the theo-drama, and she wants to conspire with Elizabeth, who has also discovered her role in the same drama. And, like Mary, we have to find our place in God's story.

Reflect: How is God working through you by means of your vocation?

_____

_____

_____

_____

_____

_____

_____

DECEMBER 23, 2024

Monday of the Fourth Week of Advent

Luke 1:57–66

When the time arrived for Elizabeth to have her child she gave birth to a son. Her neighbors and relatives heard that the Lord had shown his great mercy toward her, and they rejoiced with her. When they came on the eighth day to circumcise the child, they were going to call him Zechariah after his father, but his mother said in reply, "No. He will be called John." But they answered her, "There is no one among your relatives who has this name." So they made signs, asking his father what he wished him to be called. He asked for a tablet and wrote, "John is his name," and all were amazed. Immediately his mouth was opened, his tongue freed, and he spoke blessing God. Then fear came upon all their neighbors, and all these matters were discussed throughout the hill country of Judea. All who heard these things took them to heart, saying, "What, then, will this child be? For surely the hand of the Lord was with him."

Friends, today's Gospel celebrates the birth of John the Baptist. I think it's fair to say that you cannot really understand Jesus without understanding John, which is precisely why all four Evangelists tell the story of the Baptist as a kind of overture to the story of Jesus.

John did not draw attention to himself. Rather, he presented himself as a preparation, a forerunner, a prophet preparing the way of the Lord. He was summing up much of Israelite history, but stressing that this history was open-ended, unfinished.

And therefore, how powerful it was when, upon spying Jesus coming to be baptized, he said, "Behold, the Lamb of God." No first-century Israelite would have missed the meaning of that: behold the one who has come to be sacrificed. Behold *the* sacrifice, which will sum up, complete, and perfect the temple. Moreover, behold *the* Passover Lamb, who sums up the whole meaning of that event and brings it to fulfillment.

And this is why John says, "He must increase; I must decrease." In other words, the overture is complete, and now the great opera begins. The preparatory work of Israel is over, and now the Messiah will reign.

Reflect: In his wisdom and power, God arranged for certain people to aid in the mission of his Son, like John the Baptist. Who has God put in your life to help you fulfill the mission he has entrusted to you?

Tuesday of the Fourth Week of Advent

Luke 1:67–79

Zechariah his father, filled with the Holy Spirit, prophesied, saying:

"Blessed be the Lord, the God of Israel;
> for he has come to his people and set
>   them free.
He has raised up for us a mighty Savior,
> born of the house of his servant David.
Through his prophets he promised of old
> that he would save us from our enemies,
> from the hands of all who hate us.
He promised to show mercy to our fathers
> and to remember his holy covenant.
This was the oath he swore to our father
>   Abraham:
>   to set us free from the hand of our enemies,
>   free to worship him without fear,
>   holy and righteous in his sight
>   all the days of our life.
You, my child, shall be called the prophet of
>   the Most High,

> for you will go before the Lord to prepare
>   his way,
> to give his people knowledge of salvation
> by the forgiveness of their sins.
> In the tender compassion of our God
>   the dawn from on high shall break upon us,
>   to shine on those who dwell in darkness and
>   the shadow of death,
>   and to guide our feet into the way of peace."

Friends, today's Gospel contains the prayer of Zechariah at the birth of his son, John the Baptist.

This prayer is especially precious to priests, religious, and all those who pray the Liturgy of the Hours on a daily basis. It's called the "Benedictus," from its first word in Latin, or the "Canticle of Zechariah." What's wonderful about this prayer (and why the Church asks its ministers to pray it every day) is that it sums up magnificently the whole history of salvation, putting Jesus and John in the context of the great story of Israel.

I would like to explore two lines of that great prayer today. The God of Israel, Zechariah prays, "has come to his people and set them free." This is what God always wants to do. He hates the fact that we've become enslaved by sin and fear, and accordingly, he wants to liberate us. The central event of the Old Testament is an event of liberation from slavery. We are, as sinners, enslaved to our pride, our envy, our anger, our appetites, our greed, our lust—all of which wrap us up and keep us from being the people that we want to be.

Zechariah continues: "He has raised up for us a mighty Savior, born of the house of his servant David." God will effect this liberation through the instrumentation of a mighty Savior. This should be read against the background of Israel's long history of military struggle against its enemies. A great warrior has come, and he is from the house of Israel's greatest soldier, David. God had promised that he would put a descendant of David on the throne of Israel for all eternity, and Zechariah is prophesying that this will take place.

Reflect: The first words Zechariah spoke after being mute for more than six months were in praise of God. How often do you praise God aloud and in the presence of other people?

_____

_____

_____

_____

_____

_____

_____

_____

_____

DECEMBER 25, 2024

Solemnity of the Nativity of the Lord

John 1:1–18

In the beginning was the Word,
    and the Word was with God,
    and the Word was God.
He was in the beginning with God.
All things came to be through him,
    and without him nothing came to be.
What came to be through him was life,
    and this life was the light of the human race;
the light shines in the darkness,
    and the darkness has not overcome it.

A man named John was sent from God. He came for testimony, to testify to the light, so that all might believe through him. He was not the light, but came to testify to the light. The true light, which enlightens everyone, was coming into the world.

He was in the world,
    and the world came to be through him,
    but the world did not know him.
He came to what was his own,
    but his own people did not accept him.

But to those who did accept him he gave power to become children of God, to those who believe in his name, who were born not by natural generation nor by human choice nor by a man's decision but of God.

> And the Word became flesh
>> and made his dwelling among us,
>> and we saw his glory,
>> the glory as of the Father's only Son,
>> full of grace and truth.

John testified to him and cried out, saying, "This was he of whom I said, 'The one who is coming after me ranks ahead of me because he existed before me.'" From his fullness we have all received, grace in place of grace, because while the law was given through Moses, grace and truth came through Jesus Christ. No one has ever seen God. The only Son, God, who is at the Father's side, has revealed him.

Friends, today we celebrate the birth of Jesus Christ, the incarnate Son of God.

We hear at Mass one of the most magnificent passages in the Scriptures, indeed one of the gems of the Western literary tradition: the prologue to the Gospel of John. In many ways, the essential meaning of Christmas is contained in these elegantly crafted lines.

But today I would like to focus on how John commences: "In the beginning was the Word." No first-century Jew would have missed the significance of that opening phrase, for the first word of the Hebrew Scriptures, *bereshit*, means precisely "beginning." The evangelist is signaling that the story he will unfold is the tale of a new creation, a new beginning. The Word, he tells us, was not only *with* God from the beginning, but indeed *was* God.

Whenever we use words, we express something of ourselves. For example, as I type these words, I'm telling you what I know about the prologue to the Johannine Gospel; when you speak to a friend, you're telling him or her how you feel or what you're afraid of; when an umpire shouts out a call, he's communicating how he has assessed a play.

But God, the sheer act of Being itself, the perfect Creator of the universe, is able utterly to speak himself in one great Word, a Word that does not simply contain an aspect of his being but rather the whole of his being. This is why we say that the Word is "God from God, Light from Light, True God from True God"—and this is why St. John says that the Word was God.

Reflect: Spend some time in quiet praise and thanksgiving today for the greatest gift of all time: the incarnate Son of God!

CONCLUSION

Friends,

I'd like to thank you for journeying with me through the Advent season. Now that we've finished, you might be wondering, what's next? How do I maintain the spiritual momentum I developed this Advent? I'd like to suggest a few practical tips.

First, be sure to visit our website, wordonfire.org, on a regular basis. There you'll find lots of helpful resources, including new articles, videos, podcasts, and homilies, all designed to help strengthen your faith and evangelize the culture. The best part is that all of it is free!

In addition to those free resources, I invite you to join the Word on Fire Institute. This is an online hub of deep spiritual and intellectual formation, where you'll journey through courses taught by me and other Fellows. Our goal is to build an army of evangelists, people who have been transformed by Christ and want to bring his light to the world. Learn more and sign up at wordonfire.institute.

Finally, the best way to carry on your Advent progress is to commit to at least one new spiritual practice. For instance, you might read through one of the Gospels, one chapter per day; or start praying part of the Liturgy of the Hours; or spend some time with the Blessed Sacrament once a week; or decide to attend one extra Mass each week; or pray one Rosary each day, maybe in your car or while you exercise. All of these are simple, straightforward ways to deepen your spiritual life.

Again, thank you from all of us at Word on Fire, and God bless you during this Christmas season!

Peace,

+ Robert Barron

Bishop Robert Barron

THE
JOYFUL
MYSTERIES
OF THE ROSARY

Visit wordonfire.org/rosary for the video version.

OPENING PRAYERS

The Sign of the Cross

In the name of the Father, and of the Son, and of the
Holy Spirit. Amen.

The Apostles' Creed

I believe in God,
the Father almighty,
Creator of heaven and earth,
and in Jesus Christ, his only Son, our Lord,
who was conceived by the Holy Spirit,
born of the Virgin Mary,
suffered under Pontius Pilate,
was crucified, died, and was buried;
he descended into hell;
on the third day he rose again from the dead;
he ascended into heaven,
and is seated at the right hand of God the Father almighty;
from there he will come to judge the living and the
dead.
I believe in the Holy Spirit,
the holy catholic Church,
the communion of saints,
the forgiveness of sins,
the resurrection of the body,
and life everlasting. Amen.

The Our Father

Our Father, who art in heaven,
hallowed be thy name;
thy kingdom come,
thy will be done
on earth as it is in heaven.
Give us this day our daily bread,
and forgive us our trespasses,
as we forgive those who trespass against us;
and lead us not into temptation,
but deliver us from evil. Amen.

The Hail Mary (three times)

Hail Mary, full of grace, the Lord is with thee;
blessed art thou among women,
and blessed is the fruit of thy womb, Jesus.
Holy Mary, Mother of God,
pray for us sinners,
now and at the hour of our death. Amen.

The Glory Be

Glory be to the Father, and to the Son, and to the
    Holy Spirit;
as it was in the beginning, is now, and ever shall be,
world without end. Amen.

The First Joyful Mystery
THE ANNUNCIATION

The Annunciation focuses on the most elevated creature: Mary, the Virgin Mother of God. The angel's greeting to Mary is important: "Hail Mary, full of grace." Mary is being addressed as someone who is able to accept gifts, who is ready to receive. Then the angel announces to the maid of Nazareth that she has been chosen to be the Mother of God. Here is what Gabriel says: "Behold, you will conceive in your womb and bear a son, and you shall name him Jesus. He will be great and will be called Son of the Most High, and the Lord God will give him the throne of David his father, and he will rule over the house of Jacob forever, and of his kingdom there will be no end." No first-century Israelite would have missed the meaning here: this child shall be the fulfillment of the promise made to King David. And this means that the child is, in fact, the King of the world, the one who would bring unity and peace to all the nations. The conviction grew upon Israel that this mysterious descendant of David would be King, not just for a time and not just in an earthly sense, but forever and for all nations. This definitive King of the Jews would be King of the world. He would be our King, as well.

As we pray this decade, let us contemplate how we have allowed Jesus to be the King and Lord over our whole life.

Reflection (Short Option)

The angel Gabriel announces to Mary that she has been chosen to become the Mother of God. This child, Jesus, would be the fulfillment of the promise made to King David, ruling forever and for all nations.

The Our Father

Our Father, who art in heaven,
hallowed be thy name;
thy kingdom come,
thy will be done
on earth as it is in heaven.
Give us this day our daily bread,
and forgive us our trespasses,
as we forgive those who trespass against us;
and lead us not into temptation,
but deliver us from evil.
Amen.

The Hail Mary (ten times)

Hail Mary, full of grace, the Lord is with thee;
blessed art thou among women,
and blessed is the fruit of thy womb, Jesus.
Holy Mary, Mother of God,
pray for us sinners,
now and at the hour of our death. Amen.

The Glory Be

Glory be to the Father, and to the Son, and to the
   Holy Spirit;
as it was in the beginning, is now, and ever shall be,
world without end. Amen.

The Fatima Prayer

O my Jesus, forgive us our sins, save us from the
fires of hell; lead all souls to heaven, especially those
who have most need of thy mercy.

The Second Joyful Mystery

THE VISITATION

Reflection (Long Option)

Upon hearing the message of Gabriel concerning her own pregnancy and that of her cousin, Mary, we hear, "proceeded in haste into the hill country of Judah" to see Elizabeth.

Why did she go with such speed and purpose? Because she had found her mission, her role in the theo-drama. We are dominated today by the ego-drama in all of its ramifications and implications. The ego-drama is the play that I'm writing, I'm producing, I'm directing, and above all, that I'm starring in. We see this absolutely everywhere in our culture. Freedom of choice reigns supreme: I become the person that I choose to be. But the theo-drama is the great story being told by God, the great play being directed by God. What makes life thrilling is to discover your role in it. This is precisely what has happened to Mary. She has found her role—indeed a climactic role—in the theo-drama, and she wants to commune with Elizabeth, who has also discovered her role in that same drama.

Throughout this decade of the Rosary, let us contemplate what God reveals to us in the mystery of the Visitation. Have we searched for our place in God's story, abandoning the ego-drama for the theo-drama with a response as bold and simple as Mary's?

Reflection (Short Option)

Upon hearing the message of Gabriel, Mary "proceeded in haste" to see Elizabeth. Why did she go with such speed and purpose? Because she had found her mission, her role in the great story being told by God.

The Our Father

Our Father, who art in heaven,
hallowed be thy name;
thy kingdom come,
thy will be done
on earth as it is in heaven.
Give us this day our daily bread,
and forgive us our trespasses,
as we forgive those who trespass against us;
and lead us not into temptation,
but deliver us from evil.
Amen.

The Hail Mary (ten times)

Hail Mary, full of grace, the Lord is with thee;
blessed art thou among women,
and blessed is the fruit of thy womb, Jesus.
Holy Mary, Mother of God,
pray for us sinners,
now and at the hour of our death. Amen.

The Glory Be

Glory be to the Father, and to the Son, and to the
    Holy Spirit;
as it was in the beginning, is now, and ever shall be,
world without end. Amen.

The Fatima Prayer

O my Jesus, forgive us our sins, save us from the
fires of hell; lead all souls to heaven, especially those
who have most need of thy mercy.

The Third Joyful Mystery
THE NATIVITY

Reflection (Long Option)

When we turn to Luke's familiar account of the birth of Jesus, we see that it commences, as one would expect poems and histories in the ancient world to commence, with the invocation of powerful and important people: Emperor Augustus and Quirinius, the governor of Syria. But then Luke pulls the rug out from under us, for we promptly learn that the story isn't about Augustus and Quirinius at all, but rather about two nobodies making their way from one forgotten outpost of Augustus' empire to another. When Mary and Joseph arrived in David's city, there was no room, even at the crude travelers' hostel, and so their child is born in a cave, or as some scholars have recently suggested, the lower level of a dwelling, the humble part of the house where the animals spent the night.

Luke therefore sets up his story as the tale of two rival emperors: Caesar, the king of the world, and Jesus, the baby King. While Caesar rules from his palace in Rome, Jesus has no place to lay his head; while Caesar exercises rangy power, Jesus is wrapped in swaddling clothes; while Caesar surrounds himself with wealthy and sophisticated courtiers, Jesus is surrounded by animals and shepherds of the field. And yet, the baby King is more powerful than Augustus, which is signaled by the presence of an army (*stratias* in the Greek) of angels in the skies over Bethlehem.

All four of the Gospels play out as a struggle, culminating in the deadly business of the cross, between the worldly powers and the power of Christ. For Jesus is not simply a kindly prophet with a gentle message of forgiveness; he is God coming in person to assume command. He is the Lord, the Word made flesh.

As we pray this decade, let us contemplate the great mystery of the Nativity and the subversive presentation of the arrival of the new King.

Reflection (Short Option)

Mary and Joseph arrive in David's city and their child, the Word made flesh, is born in a cave. This is not a sentimental tale but the commencement of a great struggle between the powers of the world and the power of Christ.

The Our Father

Our Father, who art in heaven,
hallowed be thy name;
thy kingdom come,
thy will be done
on earth as it is in heaven.
Give us this day our daily bread,
and forgive us our trespasses,
as we forgive those who trespass against us;
and lead us not into temptation,
but deliver us from evil.
Amen.

The Hail Mary (ten times)

Hail Mary, full of grace, the Lord is with thee;
blessed art thou among women,
and blessed is the fruit of thy womb, Jesus.
Holy Mary, Mother of God,
pray for us sinners,
now and at the hour of our death. Amen.

The Glory Be

Glory be to the Father, and to the Son, and to the
    Holy Spirit;
as it was in the beginning, is now, and ever shall be,
world without end. Amen.

The Fatima Prayer

O my Jesus, forgive us our sins, save us from the
fires of hell; lead all souls to heaven, especially those
who have most need of thy mercy.

The Fourth Joyful Mystery

THE PRESENTATION IN THE TEMPLE

Reflection (Long Option)

The importance of this mystery is rooted in the importance of the temple for ancient Israel. The temple was, in practically a literal sense, the dwelling place of the Lord. Of all the mountains in the world, Yahweh preferred Mount Zion, and here he had chosen to live. It was the place of encounter *par excellence*. At the temple, Israel was most itself and most in touch with its mission to bring the worship of the true God to the whole world. In the temple, divinity and humanity embraced, and the human race was brought back online with God. Whenever someone offered sacrifice in the temple, he was turning his life, his mind, his will back to God. He was becoming "reconciled" ("eyelash to eyelash," from the Latin *cilia*) with the Lord.

But the sins of the nation had, according to the prophet Ezekiel, caused the glory of the Lord to depart from the temple. Therefore, one of the deepest aspirations of Israel's people was to reestablish the temple as the place of right praise so that the glory of the Lord might return. We can hear this longing in the prophets, in the Psalms, and in communities like the Essenes.

When Joseph and Mary bring the infant Jesus into the temple, therefore, we are meant to appreciate that the prophecy of Ezekiel is being fulfilled. The glory of the Lord has returned to his temple.

As we pray this decade, let us contemplate the mystery of the Presentation of the infant Jesus, God with us, here and now.

Reflection (Short Option)

Joseph and Mary bring the infant Jesus into the temple, the dwelling place of the Lord, fulfilling the prophecy that the glory of Yahweh would return to his temple.

The Our Father

Our Father, who art in heaven,
hallowed be thy name;
thy kingdom come,
thy will be done
on earth as it is in heaven.
Give us this day our daily bread,
and forgive us our trespasses,
as we forgive those who trespass against us;
and lead us not into temptation,
but deliver us from evil.
Amen.

The Hail Mary (ten times)

Hail Mary, full of grace, the Lord is with thee;
blessed art thou among women,
and blessed is the fruit of thy womb, Jesus.
Holy Mary, Mother of God,
pray for us sinners,
now and at the hour of our death. Amen.

The Glory Be

Glory be to the Father, and to the Son, and to the
    Holy Spirit;
as it was in the beginning, is now, and ever shall be,
world without end. Amen.

The Fatima Prayer

O my Jesus, forgive us our sins, save us from the
fires of hell; lead all souls to heaven, especially those
who have most need of thy mercy.

The Fifth Joyful Mystery

THE FINDING
IN THE TEMPLE

Reflection (Long Option)

After their visit to Jerusalem, Mary and Joseph, along with a bevy of their family and friends, were heading home to Nazareth. They presumed that the child Jesus was somewhere among his relatives in the caravan. Instead, he was in the temple of the Lord, conversing with the elders and masters of the Law. Distraught, Mary and Joseph spent three days looking for him. Any parent who has ever searched for a lost child knows the anguish they must have felt. Can you imagine what it was like as they tried to sleep at night, spinning out the worst scenarios in their minds?

When they finally find him, they, with understandable exasperation, upbraid him: "Child, why have you treated us like this? Look, your father and I have been searching for you in great anxiety." But Jesus responds with a kind of devastating laconicism: "Why were you searching for me? Did you not know that I must be in my Father's house?"

The story conveys a truth that runs sharply counter to our sensibilities: even the most powerful familial emotions must, in the end, give way to mission. Though she felt an enormous pull in the opposite direction, Mary let her son go, allowing him to find his.

As we pray the final decade of the Rosary, let us contemplate the paradox at the heart of this joyful mystery: that precisely in the measure that everyone in the family focuses on God's call for one another, the family becomes more loving and peaceful.

Reflection (Short Option)

After three days looking for him, Mary and Joseph find the young Jesus in the temple. Jesus says, "Did you not know that I must be in my Father's house?"—conveying that familial emotions must give way to mission.

The Our Father

Our Father, who art in heaven,
hallowed be thy name;
thy kingdom come,
thy will be done
on earth as it is in heaven.
Give us this day our daily bread,
and forgive us our trespasses,
as we forgive those who trespass against us;
and lead us not into temptation,
but deliver us from evil.
Amen.

The Hail Mary (ten times)

Hail Mary, full of grace, the Lord is with thee;
blessed art thou among women,
and blessed is the fruit of thy womb, Jesus.
Holy Mary, Mother of God,
pray for us sinners,
now and at the hour of our death. Amen.

The Glory Be

Glory be to the Father, and to the Son, and to the
    Holy Spirit;
as it was in the beginning, is now, and ever shall be,
world without end. Amen.

The Fatima Prayer

O my Jesus, forgive us our sins, save us from the
fires of hell; lead all souls to heaven, especially those
who have most need of thy mercy.

CLOSING PRAYERS

Hail, Holy Queen

Hail, holy Queen, mother of mercy,
our life, our sweetness, and our hope.
To thee do we cry, poor banished children of Eve;
to thee do we send up our sighs,
mourning and weeping in this valley of tears.
Turn, then, most gracious advocate,
thine eyes of mercy toward us;
and after this, our exile,
show unto us the blessed fruit of thy womb, Jesus.
O clement, O loving, O sweet Virgin Mary.
Pray for us, O holy Mother of God,
that we may be made worthy of the promises of Christ.
Amen.

Concluding Prayer

Let us pray.
O God, whose only begotten Son,
by his life, death, and Resurrection,
has purchased for us the rewards of eternal life,
grant, we beseech thee,
that while meditating on these mysteries
of the most holy Rosary of the Blessed Virgin Mary,
we may imitate what they contain
and obtain what they promise,
through the same Christ our Lord. Amen.

The Sign of the Cross

In the name of the Father, and of the Son, and of the Holy Spirit. Amen.